THIS or THAT?

BOOK 2

Brandon T. Snider

STERLING CHILDREN'S BOOKS

New York

STERLING CHILDREN'S BOOKS
New York

An Imprint of Sterling Publishing Co., Inc.
1166 Avenue of the Americas
New York, NY 10036

ISBN 978-1-4549-2103-5

Distributed in Canada by Sterling Publishing Co., Inc.
c/o Canadian Manda Group, 664 Annette Street
Toronto, Ontario, Canada M6S 2C8
Distributed in the United Kingdom by GMC Distribution Services
Castle Place, 166 High Street, Lewes, East Sussex, England BN7 1XU
Distributed in Australia by NewSouth Books, 45 Beach Street,
Coogee, NSW 2034, Australia

For information about custom editions, special sales,
and premium and corporate purchases, please contact Sterling Special Sales
at 800-805-5489 or specialsales@sterlingpublishing.com.

Manufactured in China

Lot #:
2 4 6 8 10 9 7 5 3 1
10/16

www.sterlingpublishing.com

Cover and interior design by Philip T. Buchanan

WOULD YOU RATHER

collect eye
BOOGERS

or

BELLY
BUTTON
CHEESE?

WOULD YOU RATHER

eat a **THIN SHELL** you find on the beach

or

Swallow a Small live **FROG?**

**WOULD
YOU RATHER**

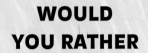

have a
weird first
name

or

have a weird
last name?

WOULD YOU RATHER be COOL to one person you really like

WORSHIPPED by one hundred people who you dislike?

WOULD YOU RATHER
be followed around by a
SMELLY OLD DOG

or

followed
around by a
**BAD TRUMPET
PLAYER?**

WOULD YOU RATHER fall off a **CLIFF**

or

get lost at **SEA?**

WOULD YOU RATHER sleep in a haunted house for one night

or

spend a day walking through a dark jungle?

WOULD YOU RATHER

accidentally text the WRONG PERSON

or

eat a terrible meal made by your BEST FRIEND?

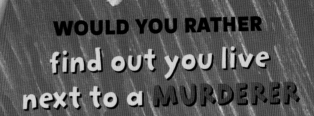

WOULD YOU RATHER find out you live next to a **MURDERER**

or

find out your parents are international **JEWEL THIEVES?**

WOULD YOU RATHER tell a child a **LIE** that makes her feel better

or

tell her the **TRUTH** knowing she'll understand it when she gets older?

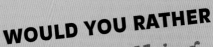

WOULD YOU RATHER

have a talking
dog who gives
you terrible
advice

a talking cat who is
good at math?

× = ÷ - + =

WOULD YOU RATHER
have your birthday on
CHRISTMAS

on
HALLOWEEN?

WOULD YOU RATHER
eat a can of
DOG FOOD

or

a can of
CAT FOOD?

WOULD YOU RATHER

have braces for
five years

or

wear headgear
for two years?

WOULD YOU RATHER flirt a lot with someone you dislike intensely

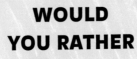

or

tell a person you love that they're ugly?

WOULD YOU RATHER

be allergic to **PIZZA**

 or

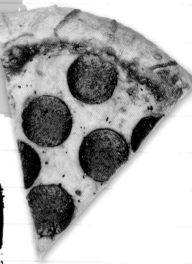

allergic to **HUGS?**

WOULD YOU RATHER
have an uncontrollable nosebleed
during a class presentation

wet your
pants
watching a
scary movie
with your
family?

WOULD YOU RATHER get a tattoo of your mom's face

or

have your mom get a tattoo of your face?

WOULD YOU RATHER

your fingers each
be a foot long

your legs
each be a
foot long?

WOULD YOU RATHER steal a bone from an **ANGRY DOG** or swim in a **LOBSTER TANK?**

WOULD YOU RATHER

lose the ability to
WALK
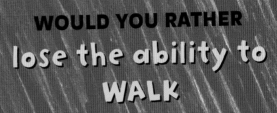

or

the ability to
HEAR?

WOULD YOU RATHER have your **TONGUE** removed

or

lose all your **HAIR?**

WOULD YOU RATHER

eat a little bit of broccoli with every meal

eat nothing but broccoli for one month straight?

WOULD YOU RATHER
wear bright RED LIPSTICK for a week

or

a long silver CAPE?

WOULD YOU RATHER

go to your first
dance with the rudest
kid in school

give one hundred
dollars to an
annoying person
who makes you feel
uncomfortable?

WOULD YOU RATHER

feed a live MOUSE
to a SNAKE

or

watch a
SEA LION get eaten
by a SHARK?

WOULD YOU RATHER

people assume everything you say is serious

assume everything you say is a joke?

WOULD YOU RATHER

gulp down a glass of sawdust

or

clean ten muddy golf balls in your mouth?

WOULD YOU RATHER
be referred to as
"MAMA'S LITTLE MUNCHKIN"

or

"PAPA'S BIG
HELPER"?

WOULD YOU RATHER feel sick to your stomach all day long

or

feel super itchy all day long and unable to scratch?

WOULD YOU RATHER

See people's
FARTS

See people's
THOUGHTS?

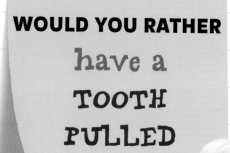

WOULD YOU RATHER have a TOOTH PULLED

or

get a SHOT?

WOULD YOU RATHER
eat MOLDY CHEESE

or

a RAW EGG?

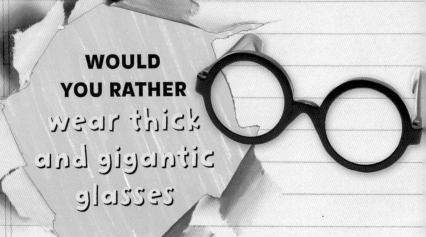

WOULD YOU RATHER *wear thick and gigantic glasses*

have your head shaved except for two pigtails?

WOULD YOU RATHER

let your friend take credit for your success

get blamed for something you didn't understand the consequences of doing?

WOULD YOU RATHER find out there was CAT POOP hidden in your pie

tiny ANT EGGS in your popcorn?

WOULD YOU RATHER

see five minutes
into the future

know a secret
about everyone
you meet?

WOULD YOU RATHER *have an ice cream* **HEADACHE**

or

a STOMACHACHE from eating too much candy?

**WOULD
YOU RATHER**
have an
extra finger
on each
hand

nostrils
the size of
quarters?

WOULD YOU RATHER discover your dad is a mean alien warlord

or

that your dad is just an actor pretending to be your dad?

WOULD YOU RATHER

grow BIRD WINGS

or

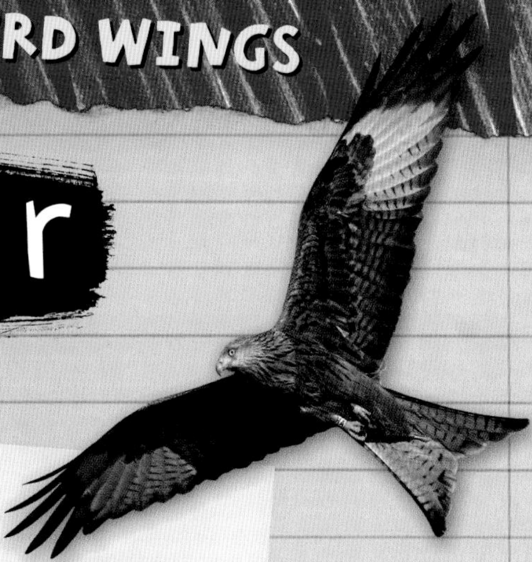

develop VAMPIRE TEETH?

WOULD YOU RATHER have an 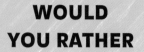**ALIEN** growing inside you

be possessed by an *EVIL SPIRIT?*

WOULD YOU RATHER

eat poop-flavored
ice cream

chew gum
that tastes
like sewage?

WOULD YOU RATHER ride a MOTORCYCLE in the rain

or

wear your BATHING SUIT in the snow?

WOULD YOU RATHER

let a dog lick your face for twenty minutes after he ate his own poop

or

swallow a spider whole?

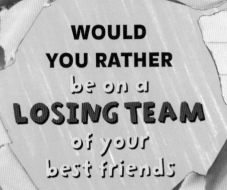

WOULD YOU RATHER be on a **LOSING TEAM** of your best friends

or

a **WINNING TEAM** of people you dislike?

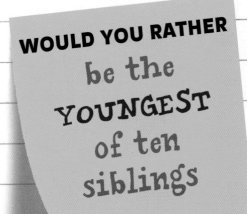

WOULD YOU RATHER
be the
YOUNGEST
of ten
siblings

or

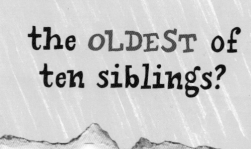

the OLDEST of
ten siblings?

WOULD YOU RATHER

wake up in a room with a
STRANGER

or

wake up in a
room with a
BULLY
from school?

WOULD YOU RATHER wash your hands in a toilet

or

a tank of barracudas?

WOULD YOU RATHER

take orders from a mean but sassy-talking bug

or

a manipulative bully from your school who promises to leave you alone?

**WOULD
YOU RATHER**

count the
grains in a
cup of sand

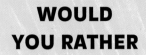

or

count the
number of hairs
on your dad's
head?

WOULD YOU RATHER

have a more ATTRACTIVE TWIN

or

a SMARTER TWIN?

WOULD YOU RATHER
eat a **CLUMP OF HAIR**
from the bathtub drain

eat a
SMALL STICK
you found
in a puddle?

WOULD YOU RATHER wear your Halloween costume to school a day late

or

give pennies away on Halloween night?

WOULD YOU RATHER

be a girl with a
boy's first name

or

a boy
with a
girl's first
name?

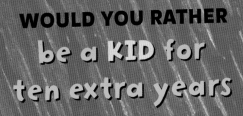

WOULD YOU RATHER
be a KID for
ten extra years

become an
ADULT
ten years early?

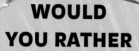

**WOULD
YOU RATHER**
be lost in the
woods by yourself
with a healthy
supply of all your
favorite
foods

in a boat ten miles
out in the ocean
with only a bag
of popcorn?

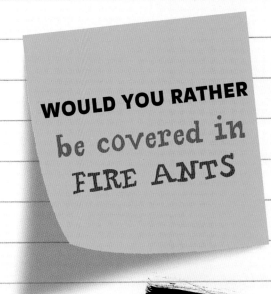

WOULD YOU RATHER

be covered in **FIRE ANTS**

or

covered in **SPIT?**

WOULD YOU RATHER

accidentally lose your best friend's favorite ring

forget to tell your mom that you got into trouble at school?

WOULD YOU RATHER
be STUNG
by ten bees

or

BITTEN
by one angry
raccoon?

WOULD YOU RATHER
have invisible skin
so everyone could see
inside you

or

have feet that itch
constantly?

WOULD YOU RATHER  eat raw **CHICKEN LIVERS**

week-old FISH HEADS?

WOULD YOU RATHER

walk everywhere you go

or

ride a crazy-looking bike wearing a sign that says "BIG KID ALERT"?

WOULD YOU RATHER
Rollerblade down a hill blindfolded

or

reach into the cushions of a dirty old couch?

WOULD YOU RATHER go on vacation to the most magical place in the universe for only one day a year

or

have your summer vacation extended by three weeks?

WOULD YOU RATHER dance around in front of a hungry bear

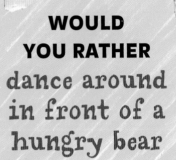

or

meow at a mountain lion?

WOULD YOU RATHER *not* BRUSH YOUR TEETH for a week

or

not take a SHOWER for a week?

WOULD YOU RATHER
be a TERRIBLE
but FAMOUS PAINTER

or

an OKAY BOWLER
who is totally
HILARIOUS?

WOULD YOU RATHER be homely until you're twenty and then become gorgeous

or

be good looking until you're thirty and then get really wrinkly?

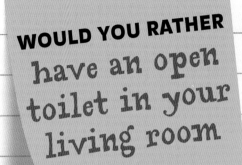

WOULD YOU RATHER have an open toilet in your living room.

or

an open shower in your front yard?

give up EATING for a week

or

give up the
INTERNET
for three
days?

WOULD YOU RATHER

eat rotting
vegetables

or

a big cup
of dry dirt?

WOULD YOU RATHER
HOLD HANDS
with someone you
DISLIKE

HUG a
Stinky
WET DOG?

WOULD YOU RATHER have the smell of **VOMIT** pumped into your bedroom at night

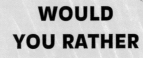

or

sit next to a person who smelled like GARBAGE all day long?

WOULD YOU RATHER run five laps around your gym backward

or

play dodgeball blindfolded?

WOULD YOU RATHER
read a book while **JOGGING**

knit a
hat on a
ROLLER COASTER?

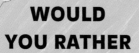

**WOULD
YOU RATHER**
convince your
class that the
**EASTER
BUNNY**
is real

or

shout "I'M IN LOVE
WITH THE TOOTH
FAIRY!" during a very
important test?

**WOULD
YOU RATHER**

forget who
your parents
are

forget all
of your
favorite
memories?

WOULD YOU RATHER

talk to people
exclusively
through
drawings

or

exclusively
through a
megaphone?

WOULD YOU RATHER

hang upside down
for one hour

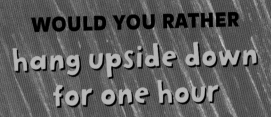

or

stay completely
still for five hours?

WOULD YOU RATHER
have to PEE every thirty minutes

or

VOMIT once a day?

WOULD YOU RATHER

know every single thing about one subject

one little thing about every subject?

WOULD YOU RATHER
tell a stranger you
"MADE A POOPY"

or

GRAB
a stranger's nose
and run away?

WOULD YOU RATHER get stuck in **QUICKSAND**

or

fall through ice into a **FREEZING LAKE?**

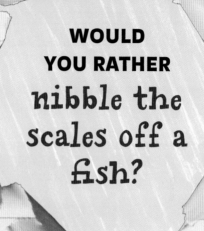

**WOULD
YOU RATHER**

nibble the
scales off a
fish?

or

stick your
tongue between
all of your
GRANDMA'S
TOES

WOULD YOU RATHER

be lucky
and dumb

or

unlucky
and very
smart?

WOULD YOU RATHER
be stuck on the top of a mountain

or

stuck at
the bottom
of a ravine?

**WOULD
YOU RATHER**
miss your sister's
school play because
you are playing
video games

or

go to an awesome
party that keeps you up
all night even though you
have to be at school early
in the morning?

WOULD YOU RATHER

grow thick black cat whiskers

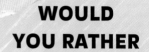

or

a giant **UNICORN** horn?

WOULD YOU RATHER
have a terrible nightmare

watch a sad movie that will make you cry?

WOULD YOU RATHER

shout **"I'M SWEATY!"** when you get nervous

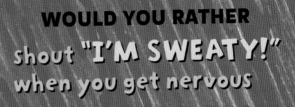

or

constantly **LICK YOUR TEETH** in a way that makes people uncomfortable?

WOULD YOU RATHER 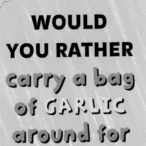 carry a bag of GARLIC around for a week

spend an entire day speaking in a really HIGH-PITCHED voice?

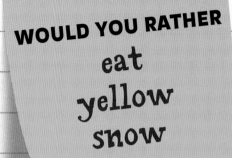

WOULD YOU RATHER
eat
yellow
snow

a piece of
chocolate that
might have
poop in it?

WOULD YOU RATHER
have BEDBUGS

or

be allergic
to the
COLD?

WOULD YOU RATHER
have a
GIANT WART
on your eyelid

or

a quarter-size
BALD SPOT
in the middle of
your head?

WOULD YOU RATHER

work as a **CLOWN** and be **RICH**

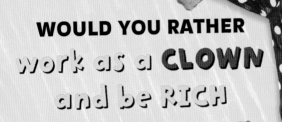

or

work as a **TEACHER** for little money and know you made a true **IMPACT** on a child's life?

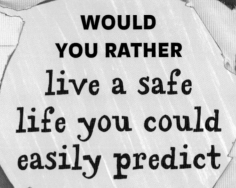

WOULD YOU RATHER live a safe life you could easily predict

or

an exciting and unpredictable life of danger?

WOULD YOU RATHER
be late to
SCHOOL

late to family
DINNER?

WOULD YOU RATHER
be SMART and UNATTRACTIVE

DUMB
and
PRETTY?

WOULD YOU RATHER tell your best friend you lost his hamster

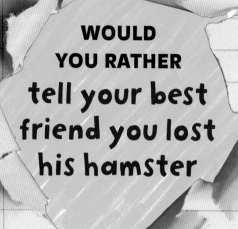

or

tell your best friend his hamster is dead?

WOULD YOU RATHER
lick a BABY'S DIRTY DIAPER

or

eat a half pound of raw ROTTING SAUSAGE?

WOULD YOU RATHER

pop your
best friend's
giant
pimple

help a toddler
walk half a
mile?

WOULD YOU RATHER
manipulate your
sibling into doing
something naughty

convince your
parents to take
you somewhere
special?

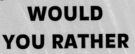

**WOULD
YOU RATHER**
study math
all day, every day,
for one year and
be done with it

or

study math
a little bit every
day for
twelve years?

WOULD YOU RATHER

try a new
and unusual
food every
single day

eat only your
favorite meal for the
rest of your life?

WOULD YOU RATHER

sleep all day

stay up all night?

WOULD YOU RATHER
pick up **DOG POOP** with your bare hand

or

write your name in a puddle of **VOMIT?**

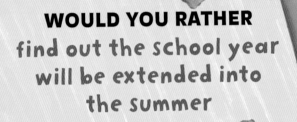

WOULD YOU RATHER
find out the school year
will be extended into
the summer

or

live somewhere
where it rains every
single day?

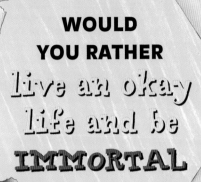

WOULD YOU RATHER live an okay life and be **IMMORTAL**

or

live a life you absolutely love and **DIE** at sixty?

WOULD YOU RATHER

have a friend who talks way too loudly in public

or

constantly stares at everyone around him?

WOULD YOU RATHER
drink a hot cup of soda

or

eat a frozen cheeseburger?

**WOULD
YOU RATHER
get a tattoo
of a butt on
your face**

**a tattoo of
a face on
your butt?**

WOULD YOU RATHER

be best friends with a STINKY SUPERMODEL

an ALL-STAR ATHLETE who shouts mean things at strangers?

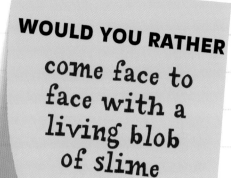

WOULD YOU RATHER

come face to
face with a
living blob
of slime

or

a giant ball
of hair
with eyes?

WOULD YOU RATHER

LOOK GREAT but feel BAD INSIDE

or

LOOK DRAB but feel GREAT INSIDE?

WOULD YOU RATHER apologize to your **MOM**

or

your **DAD?**

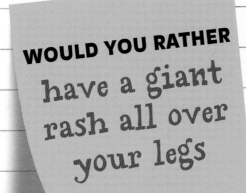

WOULD YOU RATHER have a giant rash all over your legs

a quarter-size rash on your cheek?

WOULD YOU RATHER
date someone you dislike
to become popular

date someone
you like a lot
and get labeled
an outcast?

WOULD YOU RATHER go to the **DENTIST**

or

the **DOCTOR?**

WOULD YOU RATHER beat your **SIBLING** in a board game

win an argument with your **DAD?**

WOULD YOU RATHER

be trapped on a sinking ship

or

trapped in a burning building?

WOULD YOU RATHER

be forbidden from eating your favorite food forever

only eat oatmeal with cinnamon for every meal?

WOULD YOU RATHER
see only the color PINK

smell only LASAGNA?

WOULD YOU RATHER be wanted by the **POLICE**

 or

by a bunch of scary **CRIMINALS?**

WOULD YOU RATHER

tiptoe along the top of a volcano

ride a bike in a hurricane?

WOULD YOU RATHER

poke a
stranger's
belly

get a big
wet kiss from
grandma?

WOULD YOU RATHER

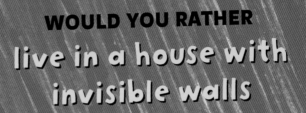

live in a house with invisible walls

or

have all your conversations broadcast on the radio?

**WOULD
YOU RATHER**
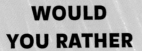
hear your
best friend
whine

or

hear your sibling
get scolded by
your parents?

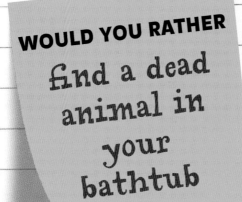

WOULD YOU RATHER

find a dead
animal in
your
bathtub

or

find a living animal
in your garage?

trip on stage in your
first acting role

or

fumble in
your first
football
game?

WOULD YOU RATHER

eat ten pounds of cheesy bacon fries

or

a bowl of raw uncooked rice?

WOULD YOU RATHER

have a friend who
hurts animals

or

a friend who is rude
and disrespectful to
elderly people?

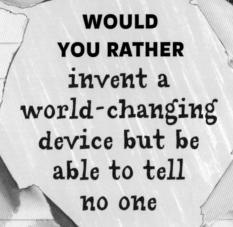

WOULD YOU RATHER invent a world-changing device but be able to tell no one

or

invent something meaningless and tell everyone?

WOULD YOU RATHER

keep a PIECE OF GLASS in your mouth

or

a POISONOUS SPIDER under your hat?

WOULD YOU RATHER
wake up at 5 a.m. every
morning for a year

graduate
high school a
year late?

WOULD YOU RATHER lose your temper in front of your parents

or

in front of a crush?

WOULD YOU RATHER

live near a toxic waste dump

near your favorite place in the whole world that you're forbidden to go to?

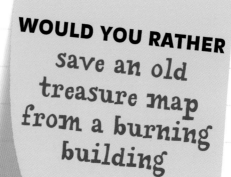

WOULD YOU RATHER
save an old treasure map from a burning building

a very old cat?

WOULD YOU RATHER

have the power of
INVISIBILITY

or

the power of
MIND CONTROL?

WOULD YOU RATHER eat a **ROTTEN APPLE**

or

eat a shish kebab of **DRY BROCCOLI?**

WOULD YOU RATHER

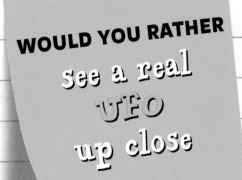

see a real
UFO
up close

or

get cornered by
BIGFOOT?

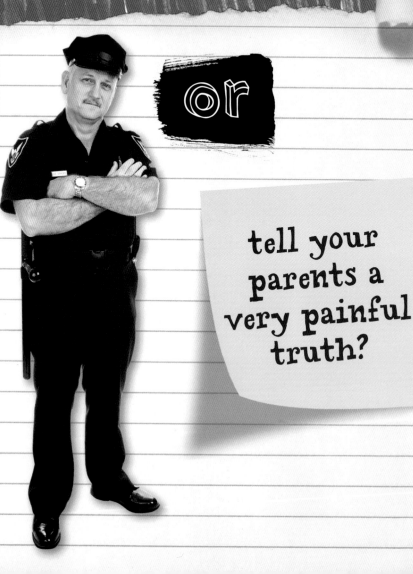

WOULD YOU RATHER

have a GHOST
for a best friend

be doomed to
a life of wearing
uncomfortable
shoes?

WOULD YOU RATHER

be able to change
one thing in your past

one thing
in your future?

**WOULD
YOU RATHER**
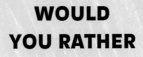
live
without the
INTERNET

or

without
RUNNING
WATER?

WOULD YOU RATHER

bring your parents along on a really special date

have your grandma watch you eat your breakfast every day for a month?

WOULD YOU RATHER
a chicken peck you
for thirty minutes

get tickled
for an hour by
someone you
dislike?

WOULD YOU RATHER have extremely large muscles that make it hard to move

or

be extremely thin with fragile bones?

WOULD YOU RATHER
tie bricks to the
bottoms of your feet
for a whole day

keep a very
loud parrot on
your shoulder
(that also poops
on you) for a
whole day?

WOULD YOU RATHER

have an uncontrollable **DROOLING PROBLEM**

an uncontrollable **BURPING PROBLEM?**

WOULD YOU RATHER

eat **SPICY MEXICAN** food and go on a **BUMPY CAR RIDE**

or

drink a gallon of **MILK** and go on a **ROLLER COASTER?**

WOULD YOU RATHER

have
skin like
STONE

or

hair like STRAW?

WOULD YOU RATHER

get a scary prank call

or

find out there was a murder in your house long ago?

WOULD YOU RATHER

live in a cave with **BATS** for a week

or

live in a closet with a **FUSSY SIBLING** for a month?

WOULD YOU RATHER

dive into an
ICE-COLD POOL

or

eat a jar of
peanut butter mixed
with HAIR?

WOULD YOU RATHER

be late to a big math test

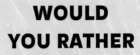

be late to a very important family event?

WOULD YOU RATHER get lost in a pitch-black forest

or

wait to be rescued for 24 hours on a snowy mountain in a blizzard?

WOULD YOU RATHER
eat a handful of crickets

or

one humongous bag of powdered sugar?

WOULD YOU RATHER have **ONE WISH** to save the world

or

TEN WISHES to save only yourself?

WOULD YOU RATHER

be color-blind

have no
eyebrows?

WOULD YOU RATHER

carry around
a thermos
that says
"BABY'S MAGIC
JUICY JUICE"

wear a hat that says
"ASK ME ABOUT
MY HUGGY
BEAR"?

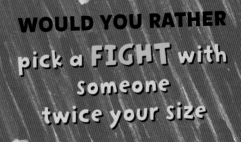

WOULD YOU RATHER

pick a **FIGHT** with someone twice your size

or

get cornered by an ANGRY BADGER?

WOULD YOU RATHER

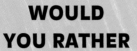

take back something you said and didn't mean

have the courage to say something you wouldn't normally say?

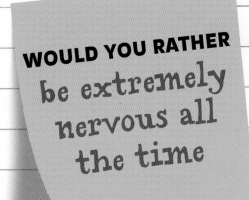

WOULD YOU RATHER
be extremely nervous all the time

or

constantly exhausted and tired?

WOULD YOU RATHER

lick a TOILET SEAT

or

lick a
BATHROOM
FLOOR?

WOULD YOU RATHER

be hit with
hundreds of tiny
pebbles

or

one big
bowling ball?

WOULD YOU RATHER

regret telling someone you love them

or

regret not telling someone how they hurt you?

WOULD YOU RATHER ask a mean-looking stranger for directions

ask your teacher for a kiss?

WOULD YOU RATHER have no fingernails

or

regular fingernails except for one that is two feet long?

WOULD YOU RATHER
eat a cake that was made with
HUMAN BLOOD

or

drink
lemonade
that has a
SPOONFUL
OF PEE
in it?

WOULD YOU RATHER have your pants pulled down in front of a crush

wear a skimpy bathing suit for a whole day?

WOULD YOU RATHER
do a super heroic
deed no one will
ever know about

a lame thing
everyone will
know about?

WOULD YOU RATHER

get caught
laughing
hysterically
at a funeral

start crying
uncontrollably
during a school
assembly?

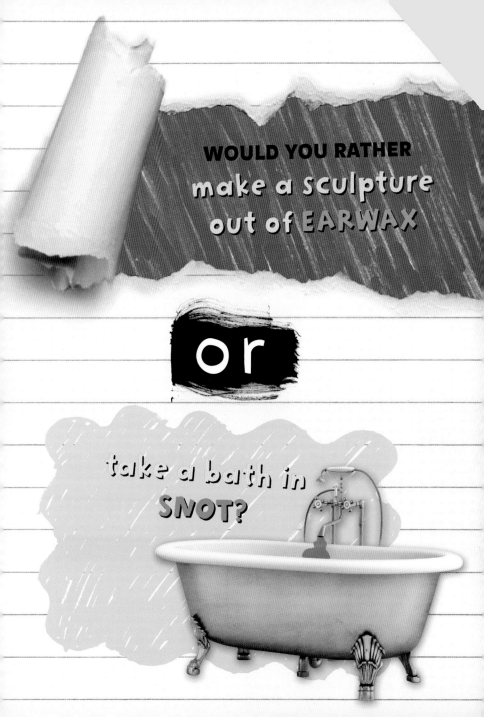

WOULD YOU RATHER 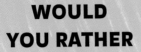 be **HAPPY** and **HOMELESS**

MISERABLE in the **HOUSE OF YOUR DREAMS?**

WOULD YOU RATHER *juggle* DOG POOP

or

juggle FLAMING KNIVES?

WOULD YOU RATHER
catch a burglar breaking
into your house

or

catch a
classmate
stealing from
your best
friend?

WOULD YOU RATHER

spend a year in a
hot-air balloon

or

spend a year
in a basement
with no
sunlight?

WOULD YOU RATHER
have your parachute
malfunction mid-jump
from a plane

run out of air on
a deep-sea dive?

**WOULD
YOU RATHER**

eat a pound
of DANDRUFF

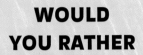

rub a pound of
RAT DROPPINGS
all over your face?

WOULD YOU RATHER dye your hair white

or

wear a mustache made of your dad's hair?

WOULD YOU RATHER
squeeze dirty sponge juice
into your mouth

or

lick the
backseat of
a New York
City taxi?

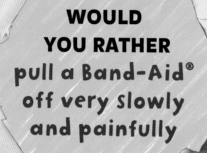

WOULD YOU RATHER pull a Band-Aid® off very slowly and painfully

or

get pricked by a hundred tiny needles all over your body?

WOULD YOU RATHER

sniff a
STRANGER'S
ARMPIT

or

sniff a
STRANGER'S
BUTT?

WOULD YOU RATHER

hug a clammy
weirdo for one
full minute

stick your hand
in a garbage bag
filled with a
slimy unknown
substance?

WOULD YOU RATHER

walk five miles a day for water

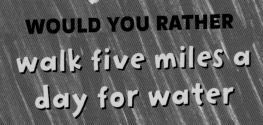

or

walk five miles a day for twenty pounds of whatever kind of candy you wanted?

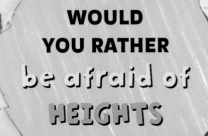

**WOULD
YOU RATHER**
be afraid of
HEIGHTS

or

afraid of
SMALL SPACES?

WOULD YOU RATHER

listen to your least favorite type of music for twenty-four hours straight

only listen to one song for the rest of your life?

WOULD YOU RATHER

have a visible face rash for a week

or

wear the same socks for a month?

WOULD YOU RATHER
eat the same thing every day, for every meal, for the rest of your life

or

eat a completely different thing every day, for every meal, for the rest of your life?

WOULD YOU RATHER

have the world's most
OBNOXIOUS LAUGH

or

a major
FARTING PROBLEM?

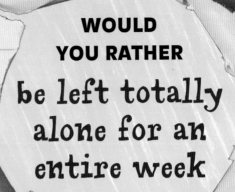

WOULD YOU RATHER

be left totally alone for an entire week

or

spend four days with ten family members in a one-bedroom house?

WOULD YOU RATHER find out you have a monkey's heart

or

find out you were molded from clay and brought to life with magic?

WOULD YOU RATHER
have **THREE** really
BORING SUPERPOWERS

or

ONE very **COOL**
SUPERPOWER
you can only
use once a
month?

WOULD YOU RATHER move to a new town every year

or

stay in the same town for the rest of your life?

WOULD YOU RATHER

find out your
crush is a
total slob

find out your
best friend
is hiding
something
from you?

WOULD YOU RATHER be strapped to a semitruck going full speed down the highway

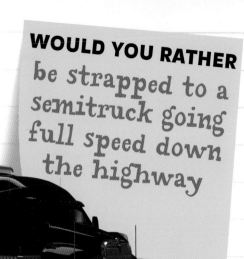

or

walk a five-foot-long tightrope that's ten stories high?

WOULD YOU RATHER

discover a lost city hidden under your house that you have to keep a secret

or

find one thousand dollars on the street?

**WOULD
YOU RATHER**
have your worst
enemy blow hot
onion breath in
your face for
five minutes

let ten cute
poop-covered puppies
jump all over you for
ten minutes?

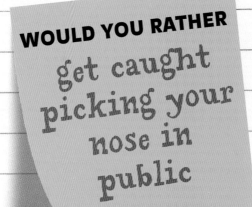

WOULD YOU RATHER

get caught
picking your
nose in
public

or

get caught eating
a booger in private?

WOULD YOU RATHER

wear a wet dog food helmet

or

a beard
made of
cat hair?

WOULD YOU RATHER

marry a **MILLIONAIRE** who treats you **BADLY**

someone who doesn't have any money but treats you with love and **RESPECT?**

WOULD YOU RATHER

have hair like the
end of a BROOM

a TINY SIXTH FINGER
located in the palm
of your hand?